SPACE MATH

Math and My World

Kieran Walsh

Rourke
Publishing LLC
Vero Beach, Florida 32964

www.rourkepublishing.com

PHOTO CREDITS:
All photos from AbleStock.com

Editor: Frank Sloan

Library of Congress Cataloging-in-Publication Data

Walsh, Kieran.
  Space math / Kieran Walsh.
      p. cm. -- (Math and my world II)
  Includes index.
  ISBN 1-59515-494-9 (hardcover)
  1. Arithmetic--Juvenile literature. 2. Outer space--Juvenile literature.
I. Title II. Series: Walsh, Kieran. Math and my world II.

  QA115.W274 2006
  513--dc22
                                    2005015007

Printed in the USA
w/w

TABLE OF CONTENTS

INTRODUCTION

Have you ever tried to count the stars? It's hard to do. You can count up pretty high, but eventually you lose track of where you started. Space, just like the number of stars that fill it, is infinite. It goes on and on... and on!

You can explore space just by looking through a telescope!

For as long as human beings have lived, we've been fascinated by the stars and planets that exist in outer space. The exciting thing about being alive today is that we actually have the technology to leave the earth and explore these other planets. The human race is many thousands of years old, but we have only just begun to explore space.

What we'll find out there is a fantastic mystery. Maybe we'll meet other forms of life. Maybe we'll find other planets that the human race can colonize. Maybe we'll discover the origins of the universe!

In this book you'll see how math helps scientists to understand space, the size of the solar system we live in, and conditions on other planets. If you're interested in studying outer space, or maybe even other planets, you're going to need to know your math. As you will see, math is a large part of what makes space exploration possible!

THE MOON

July 20, 1969 is an important date for the entire human race. It was on this day that a human being first walked on the surface of another planet—the moon.

Assuming that you are reading this book in 2006, can you calculate how many years have passed since the Apollo 11 moon landing?

The Apollo 11 mission that put men on the moon is one of the most extraordinary achievements of the human race.

To find the answer, just subtract the smaller number from the larger number:

$$2006 - 1969 = 37$$

It has been 37 years since the Apollo 11 moon landing!

For years, people had watched the moon in the sky and wondered what it was really like. The fact that human beings were able to find a way to actually journey to the moon and set foot on it is nothing less than astounding.

Our planet Earth **revolves** around a much larger body, the sun. The same pattern follows with the earth and the moon. As the smaller body, the moon orbits around the earth. Because it is always in motion, the moon is never precisely the same distance from the earth. When it is closest, the moon is about 227,000 miles from the earth. When it is farthest away, the moon is about 254,000 miles from the earth.

When the moon is closest to the earth, the distance between them is about 227,000 miles. Since there are 5,280 feet in one mile, how many feet is that?

Using those figures, let's calculate the average distance from the earth to the moon.

An **average** is a number that represents a group of numbers. For instance, do your parents give you an allowance? Maybe they give you some money each week for the different chores you do around the house.

Let's say that your allowance for three weeks is:

Week 1 = $2.50

Week 2 = $3.85

Week 3 = $1.20

Based on those numbers, what would your average weekly allowance be?

You can find out in two steps. First, add all the different amounts together:

$$2.50 + 3.85 + 1.20 = 7.55$$

The next step is to divide the result (7.55) by the number of **addends**. The addends are the numbers you added together. In this case, there were three addends, 2.50, 3.85, and 1.20:

$$7.55 \div 3 = 2.51$$

So now you can say that your average allowance for each of those three weeks was $2.51!

Now try the same thing with the distance from the earth to the moon:

$$227{,}000 + 254{,}000 = 481{,}000$$
$$481{,}000 \div 2 = 240{,}500$$

The average distance between the earth and the moon is approximately 240,500 miles!

The moon actually has several looks, or phases.
Pictured here is what is called a "crescent" moon.

Just for comparison, consider the distance between two major American cities. The distance between New York on the east coast of the United States and Los Angeles on the west coast is roughly 3,000 miles.

How does that compare with the distance from the earth to the moon?

One way to find out is to subtract the smaller number from the larger number:

$$240,500 - 3,000 = 237,500$$

The distance from the earth to the moon is 237,500 miles greater than the distance between New York and Los Angeles!

There is another way you can compare these two numbers, though. You can do this by using **multiples**.

You may have noticed that the word "multiples" sounds a lot like *multiplication*. That's because any number being multiplied produces multiples. For instance, multiply the number five by some common **integers**:

$$0 \times 5 = 0$$
$$1 \times 5 = 5$$
$$2 \times 5 = 10$$

The answers, 0, 5, and 10, are all multiples of 5!

Now consider these numbers:

6   24

What would you have to multiply the number 6 by to give the product 24? You can find out by using division:

$$24 \div 6 = 4$$

Supposedly the computers on board the Apollo 11 only had the processing power of a modern pocket calculator!

Multiplying 6 by 4 gives 24. Another thing you can say here, though, is that the product 24 is *four times as great* as six!

Let's do the same thing with the two distances:

$$240{,}500 \div 3{,}000 = 80.16$$

The distance from the earth to the moon is about 80 times as great as the distance from New York to Los Angeles!

Liftoff!

July 20 is the date that the first human being walked on another planet. The Apollo 11 journey, though, had actually begun 4 days earlier on July 16. This was the date the **astronauts** blasted off the launch pad at Cape Kennedy in Florida.

If it took 4 days for the astronauts to cover a distance of roughly 240,500 miles, about how fast were they traveling?

To find out, you'll need to know that there are 24 hours in a day. First, find out how many hours there are in 4 days:

$$4 \times 24 = 96$$

There are 96 hours in 4 days!

Now divide the distance of the trip by the number of hours:

$$240{,}500 \div 96 = 2505.20$$

The astronauts traveled to the moon at a speed of roughly 2,500 miles per hour!

Most of this rocket will not actually travel into space. Rather, the bottom portions merely push the space capsule on top out of Earth's field of gravity.

THE SOLAR SYSTEM

The earth and the moon are part of a much larger group of planets, all of them in **orbit** around the sun. That is why we call this cluster of planets our solar system.

In our solar system there are nine planets:

Mercury

Venus

Earth

Mars

Jupiter

Saturn

Uranus

Neptune

Pluto

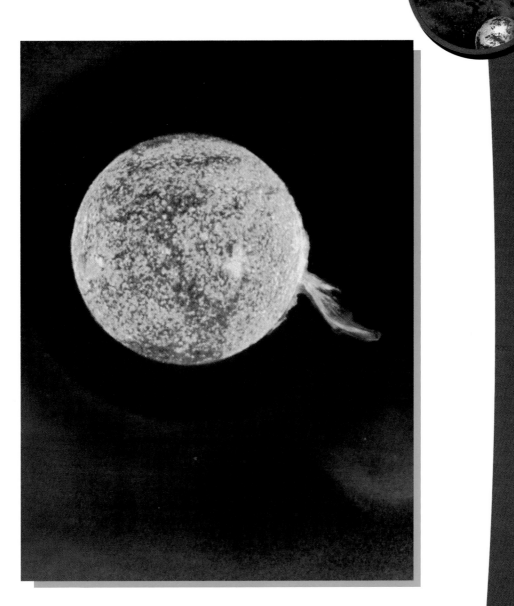

Earth is just one of several planets that revolve around the massive fireball we call the sun.

The planet Earth is a big place. Currently, it supports a population of more than 6 billion human beings. The planet Earth, though, is not the largest planet in the solar system. In order to understand planet sizes, you need to know a little about **diameter**.

If someone asked you to measure the length of your bed, you could do it by using a tape measure or even a ruler. But what if someone asked you to measure the *length* of a basketball?

The length of a round object has to be measured in terms of diameter.

A round object needs to be measured somewhat differently than a flat object. This is done, in a sense, by thinking of the round object as flat. For instance, measuring the length of that basketball would be tricky. But measuring something round *and* flat, like a pizza, wouldn't be too hard. All you would need to do is put a ruler over the pizza and find the distance between two points on the crust. To make sure that you were measuring the longest distance between two points on the pizza, you would make sure that the ruler passed over the center of the pizza.

This is how diameter works. The definition of diameter is the distance between two points on the **circumference**, or edge, of a circle and passing through the center of the circle. Diameter is how we measure the size of a planet.

The earth has a diameter of about 7,927 miles. Just for reference, the moon has a diameter of about 2,160 miles.

To make things easier, let's round off those numbers. We can say that the earth has a diameter of roughly 8,000 miles and the moon has a diameter of 2,000 miles.

How would you compare these two distances?

For one thing, you can subtract the smaller number from the larger number:

$$8,000 - 2,000 = 6,000$$

The earth's diameter is roughly 6,000 miles greater than the diameter of the moon!

Another way to compare these distances, though, is to use multiples:

$$8,000 \div 2,000 = 4$$

The earth's diameter is roughly 4 times greater than the diameter of the moon. Or, to put it another way, the moon's diameter is about 1/4 (one quarter) that of the earth!

Jupiter, the largest of the nine planets in our solar system

Let's look at the list of planets in our solar system again. This time, though, we're going to include the diameter (in miles) of each planet:

Mercury – 3,049
Venus – 7,565
Earth – 7,927
Mars – 4,243
Jupiter – 89,500
Saturn – 75,000
Uranus – 32,125
Neptune – 30,938
Pluto – 1,875

The number that probably caught your attention is the diameter for Jupiter. As you can see, Jupiter is *huge*. How much bigger is Jupiter than the earth?

$$89{,}500 - 7{,}927 = 81{,}573$$

The diameter of Jupiter is about 81,573 miles greater than that of the earth!

Another way to express this would be to use multiples like you did with the earth and the moon. Just divide the larger number by the smaller number:

$$89{,}500 \div 7{,}927 = 11.29$$

Jupiter is roughly 11 times the size of the earth!

On the other end of the scale there is Pluto. Pluto is the planet farthest away from the sun. It is also the smallest planet in the solar system.

How much bigger is the earth compared to Pluto? Express the answer in terms of multiples.

$$7{,}927 \div 1{,}875 = 4.22$$

The earth is about 4 times the size of Pluto!

Here's a question. What is the largest object in our solar system?

Maybe you said Jupiter. It seems like the obvious answer, considering Jupiter's massive size. However, there is a much larger object in the solar system…

The sun!

Compared to the sun, even gigantic Jupiter looks tiny. The diameter of the sun is estimated to be about 864,000 miles! How does that compare with Jupiter?

$$864{,}000 \div 89{,}500 = 9.65$$

We can say two things with this result. First, we can say that the sun is roughly 10 times the size of Jupiter. We can also say that Jupiter is about 1/10 (one tenth) the size of the sun!

How does the earth compare with the sun?

$$864,000 \div 7,927 = 108.9$$

The sun is about 109 times the size of the earth!

The earth's moon is a satellite, but satellites can also be man-made structures like this space station.

Satellites

Our solar system also includes a multitude of smaller planets that orbit the nine major planets. These smaller planets are sometimes called **satellites.** The planet Earth has only 1 satellite, the moon. Other planets have many, many more. Uranus, for instance, has 15 satellites. How many more satellites does Uranus have compared to Earth?

$$15 - 1 = 14$$

Uranus has 14 more satellites than planet Earth!

ASTRONOMICAL UNITS

Now that you have looked at the sizes of the different planets and even the sun, you may be wondering how big the entire solar system is.

This is sort of a tricky question. It depends on what we consider to be the **boundary** of the solar system. Although some scientists prefer to reach further into space, let's say for now that the end of our solar system is the last planet, Pluto.

Our solar system resides in the Milky Way Galaxy, which is shaped like a spiral.

The size of Jupiter, even the size of the sun, is nothing compared to the vast distances between planets. These lengths are so gigantic that scientists even developed a measurement to deal with them. These are known as **astronomical units** (AU).

One astronomical unit is the distance from the sun to the earth, which is about 92.9 million miles. 92.9 million miles is equal to 1 AU.

Pluto is 39.4 AU from the sun. Remember that diameter is like a line connecting two opposite points on a circle and passing through the center. So imagine that the distance from the sun to Pluto is half of a diameter line. In order to calculate the diameter of our solar system, you have to multiply the distance from the sun to Pluto by 2:

$$39.4 \times 2 = 78.8$$

Our solar system is approximately 79 AU! Can you express that in miles? All you have to do is multiply the measurement in astronomical units by the number of miles in one AU:

$$79 \times 92,900,000 = 7,339,100,000$$

Our solar system is more than 7 *billion* miles in diameter!

Now that you have some knowledge of astronomical units, you can examine how far other planets are from Earth.

Here is a list of the nine major planets and their distances from the sun:

Mercury – .04 AU
Venus – .07 AU
Earth – 1 AU
Mars – 1.5 AU
Jupiter – 5.2 AU
Saturn – 9.6 AU
Uranus – 19.2 AU
Neptune – 30.1 AU
Pluto – 39.4 AU

It has been years since a manned mission to another planet like the Apollo 11 program was attempted. Usually when a new mission is discussed, the proposed destination is the "red planet," Mars.

The surface of Mars appears red because it is composed of rusting iron.

If Mars is 1.5 AU from the sun, and Earth is 1 AU from the sun, how far is Mars from Earth?

$$1.5 - 1 = .5 \text{ AU}$$

Mars is approximately .5 AU from Earth. How many miles is that?

$$92,900,000 \times .5 = 46,450,000$$

Mars is about 46 million miles from Earth!

For a moment imagine that a journey to Mars was attempted using a vehicle like the one in which the Apollo 11 crew traveled. Earlier, we calculated that the Apollo 11 astronauts traveled to the moon at a speed of 2,500 mph. How long would it take astronauts to reach Mars at that speed?

$$46,450,000 \div 2,500 = 18,580$$

18,580 hours! How many days is that?

$$18,580 \div 24 = 774.1$$

About 774 days!

If there are 365 days in a year, how many years would it take the astronauts to reach Mars?

$$774 \div 365 = 2.12$$

2 years!

2 years is a long time, but bear in mind that those calculations were done using the speed of a craft that was built almost 40 years ago. If a mission to Mars was undertaken now, it would use ships that could travel at much greater speed. Most scientists imagine a journey time of mere months. Some think the journey could be made in as little as 6 months.

The Space Shuttle is currently the state of the art in spaceships, but newer, more efficient crafts will need to be developed for long-distance space travel. ▶

For a crew of astronauts to travel to Mars in just 6 months, how fast would their ship have to go?

First, convert 6 months into hours. You know that there are 365 days in a year. You also know that there are 12 months in one year. So, if 6 months is equal to half of one year, how many days is that? You can find out by dividing the number of days in one year by 2:

$$365 \div 2 = 182.5$$

The number of days in 6 months is 183! If there are 24 hours in a day, how many hours are there in 183 days?

$$24 \times 183 = 4,392$$

There are 4,392 hours in 183 days!

To find out the speed at which astronauts will have to travel to reach Mars in 6 months, divide the distance (in miles) from Earth to Mars by the number of hours in 6 months:

$$46,450,000 \div 4,392 = 10,576.04$$

The astronauts would be traveling at roughly 10,600 miles per hour!

Light-Years

A unit of measurement closely related to astronomical units is the **light-year**, also known as the **astron**.

Light-years are a measurement of the distance traveled by light in a single year, or 365 days. The approximate measure of a light-year is roughly 5.88 trillion miles, or:

5,880,000,000,000 miles!

Light-years are used when measuring distances that even astronomical units are too small for. Just one example is the distance between our sun and the closest other sun in our galaxy, Alpha Centauri. This is a distance of 4.3 light-years.

Can you calculate how many miles that is?

25,284,000,000,000 miles!

GRAVITY

The orbits of the planets are created by the same force that causes a football to fall back to the earth after it's been kicked high into the air. We call this force **gravity**.

How much do you weigh? Whatever the number is, you probably expressed your weight in terms of pounds. Did you know that pounds are actually a measurement of force? Pounds are a measure of how much "pull" that gravity has on an object.

Legend has it that Sir Isaac Newton "discovered" gravity after an apple fell on his head.

If you have ever tried to pick up a heavy object, you know that some things are heavier than others. An encyclopedia volume is heavier than a birthday card. A rock is heavier than a pine cone.

One of the reasons why some objects weigh more than others is size. A car is heavier than a bicycle because it is much bigger. Another reason why weight varies, though, is because of **mass**.

Imagine two objects that are about the same in terms of size. Take, for example, a baseball bat made from wood and a baseball bat made out of plastic. If they are both roughly the same size, then why does the baseball bat made from wood weigh more than the bat made out of plastic? The answer is that the wooden bat has more mass.

The reason why this anvil is heavy is because it has so much mass. An object of the same size made out of styrofoam would weigh much less.

Mass is a word that describes the amount of matter contained in an object. Objects with more mass weigh more because they have more matter for gravity to "pull" on. This is why a brick weighs more than a piece of wood that is the same size.

When Neil Armstrong and "Buzz" Aldrin first walked on the moon more than 30 years ago, they were protected by space suits that included special weighted boots. This was to compensate for the fact that the moon has far less gravitational pull than the earth. It makes perfect sense if you remember that the moon is about 1/4 the size of planet Earth!

The moon's gravitational pull is roughly 1/6 (one-sixth) that of the earth. If an object weighs 60 pounds on the earth, how much would it weigh on the moon?

Without their weighted boots, the astronauts who walked on the moon would have floated off into space! ▶

Before you do any calculations, look at the number used to compare the moon's gravitational pull to that of the earth—1/6. 1/6 is a **fraction**. Fractions are, in a way, a kind of hidden division problem. Fractions are made up of two numbers. The number above the bar is called the **numerator**. The number below the bar is the **denominator**. To find the value of a fraction, you need to divide the numerator by the denominator:

$$1 \div 6 = 0.16$$

So, to find out how much a 60-pound object weighs on the moon, you just need to multiply the weight of the object by 0.16:

$$60 \times 0.16 = 9.6$$

An object that weighs 60 pounds on Earth would weigh about 10 pounds on the moon!

So far in the history of our race, humans have only traveled to one other planet. In the distant future, though, people are sure to visit other neighbors in our solar system. All of the different planets have different sizes and masses. What kind of weights will people encounter on them?

Here's a chart that you can use to calculate weights on the nine planets in our solar system:

Mercury - 0.4
Venus - 0.9
Earth - 1
Mars - 0.4
Jupiter - 2.5
Saturn - 1.1
Uranus - 0.8
Neptune - 1.2
Pluto - 0.01

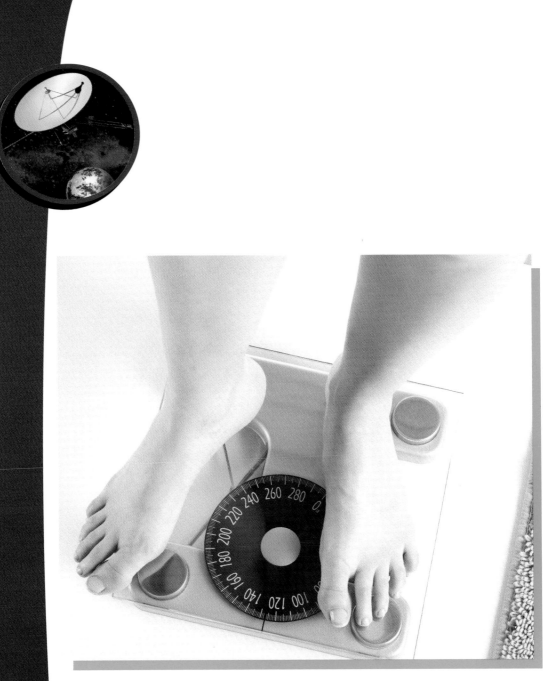

How much would you weigh on other planets?

Suppose a person weighs 150 pounds on Earth. How much would that person weigh on Mars? To find out, you only have to multiply the earth weight by the number next to the planet you're calculating for:

$$150 \times 0.4 = 60$$

A person who weighs 150 pounds on Earth would weight about 60 pounds on Mars!

How much would that same person weigh on Jupiter?

$$150 \times 2.5 = 375$$

375 pounds!

How much would that person weigh on the smallest planet in our solar system, Pluto?

$$150 \times 0.01 = 1.5$$

A person who weighs 150 pounds on Earth would only weigh 1.5 pounds on Pluto. Any astronauts visiting Pluto are going to need some very heavy boots!

The Tides

Not all of the gravity that affects our lives originates on Earth. For instance, the **tides** that pound our beaches with water are a result of the gravitational force of the moon. Tides are the rise and fall of bodies of water. If you think of this in terms of the moon's gravity, the tides are just being pulled into the air by the moon. The first person to discover this was Isaac Newton, who also "discovered" gravity!

Think about the moon the next time you watch the tides crash on the beach! ▶

CONCLUSION

Now that you have some knowledge of how space exploration and math are related, you probably have a lot more respect for all the work that goes into a space mission. You now have a better understanding of all the work and preparation that is needed for a safe and successful journey.

Maybe you'll want to consider becoming an astronaut. You could be one of the first humans to walk on Mars!

How old are you now? Imagine that the first manned mission to Mars takes place in 2024. How many years do you have to wait to go to Mars?

Study hard, and one day you could be an astronaut!

THE METRIC SYSTEM

We actually have two systems of weights and measures in the United States. Quarts, pints, gallons, ounces, and pounds are all units of the U.S. Customary System, also known as the English System.

The other system of measurement, and the only one sanctioned by the United States Government, is the metric system, which is also known as the International System of Units. French scientists developed the **metric** system in the 1790s. The basic unit of measurement in the metric system is the **meter**, which is about one ten-millionth the distance from the North Pole to the equator.

A metal bar used to represent the length of the standard meter was even created. This bar was replaced in the 1980s, though, when scientists changed the standard of measurement for the meter to a portion of the distance traveled by light in a vacuum.

The metric system can be applied to space and space travel in an infinite number of ways. For instance, you learned that the average distance from the earth to the moon is about 240,500 miles. In the metric system, that distance would be measured in terms of kilometers. Converting miles to kilometers is easy. All you have to do is multiply the number of miles by 1.6. So, how many kilometers are there between the earth and the moon?

$$240{,}500 \times 1.6 = 384{,}800$$

The moon is roughly 385,000 kilometers from the earth!

Remember that the nearest star, Alpha Centauri, is 25,284,000,000,000 miles from the sun. How many kilometers is that?

Another area where you can apply the metric system measurements is weight. The basic unit of mass in the metric system is the kilogram. In order to convert from pounds to kilograms, you must multiply the pound measurement by 0.45. So, if an astronaut weighs 175 pounds on Earth, how many kilograms is that?

$$175 \times 0.45 = 78.75$$

About 79 kilograms!

How many kilograms would that astronaut weigh on Mars?

$$79 \times 0.45 = 35.55$$

An astronaut who weighs roughly 79 kilograms on Earth would weigh about 35 kilograms on Mars!

The metric system is pretty easy once you get the hang of it. For practice, you could go through this book and convert some of the numbers to metric.

Try it!

GLOSSARY

addends — the numbers added together in an addition problem

astron — another word for light-year

astronauts — those trained to be a pilot or crew member of a spacecraft

astronomical units — measurements used to chart distances in outer space

average — a number used to represent a group of numbers

boundary — the outer limit of something

circumference — the edge, or outline of a circle

denominator — the bottom number of a fraction

diameter — the length of a straight line passing through a circle

fraction — another way of writing a division problem; a number composed of two numbers

gravity — the invisible force that attracts smaller bodies to a planet

integers — numbers

light-year — the distance traveled by light in one year

mass — the amount of matter an object has

meter — about 39.37 inches; one ten-millionth the distance from the North Pole to the equator

metric — the system of measurement used by most of the world; the International System of Units

multiples — the results of multiplying a single number by a series of other numbers

numerator — the top number of a fraction

orbit — the path of a body in space as it revolves around another, larger body

revolves — spins; rotates

satellites — bodies that orbit a planet

tides — the rise and fall of bodies of water

Further Reading

Slavin, Steve. *All the Math You'll Ever Need.* John Wiley and Sons, Inc. 1999.

Zeman, Anne and Kate Kelly. *Everything You Need to Know About Math Homework.* Scholastic, 1994.

Zeman, Anne and Kate Kelly. *Everything You Need to Know About Science Homework.* Scholastic, 1994.

Websites to Visit

http://www.pbs.org/teachersource/mathline/concepts/space.shtm
PBS Teacher Source – Mathline, Space

http://www.hypertextbook.com/facts/2004/StevenMai.shtml
Hypertextbook – Diameter of the Solar System

http://library.thinkquest.org/CR0215468/apollo_11.htm
Think Quest – Apollo 11

INDEX

ABOUT THE AUTHOR

Kieran Walsh has written a variety of children's nonfiction books, primarily on historical and social studies topics, including the Rourke series *Holiday Celebrations* and *Countries in the News*. He lives in New York City.